BELiEVE iN YOUR SELF

summersdale

BELIEVE IN YOURSELF

This edition copyright © Summersdale Publishers Ltd, 2019
First published in 2015

Research by Kristina Adamson

An Hachette UK Company
www.hachette.co.uk

Summersdale Publishers Ltd
Part of Octopus Publishing Group Limited
Carmelite House
50 Victoria Embankment
LONDON
EC4Y 0DZ

www.summersdale.com

Printed and bound in China

ISBN: 978-1-78685-803-0

Substantial discounts on bulk quantities of Summersdale books are available to corporations, professional associations and other organizations. For details contact general enquiries: telephone: +44 (0) 1243 771107 or email: enquiries@summersdale.com.

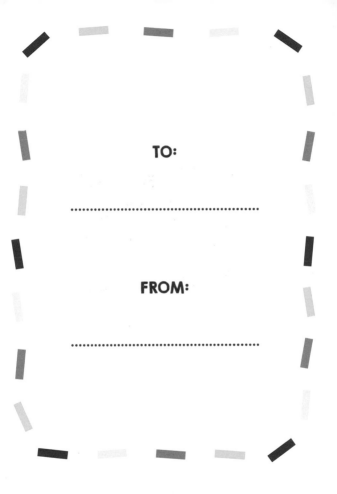

TO:

....

FROM:

....

BE YOURSELF. THE WORLD WORSHIPS THE ORIGINAL.

Ingrid Bergman

DO WHAT YOU CAN, WITH WHAT YOU'VE GOT, WHERE YOU ARE.

Squire Bill Widener

Nothing is impossible when you believe in yourself

YOU'RE PERFECT WHEN YOU'RE COMFORTABLE BEING YOURSELF.

Ansel Elgort

DO A LITTLE
MORE EACH
DAY THAN YOU
THINK YOU
POSSIBLY CAN.

LOWELL THOMAS

I DON'T WANT
OTHER PEOPLE
TO DECIDE
WHO I AM.
I WANT TO
DECIDE THAT
FOR MYSELF.

EMMA WATSON

EVEN IF
YOU FALL ON
YOUR FACE,
YOU'RE STILL
MOVING
FORWARD.

VICTOR KIAM

EXPECT PROBLEMS AND EAT THEM FOR BREAKFAST.

ALFRED A. MONTAPERT

WHAT YOU PLANT NOW, YOU WILL HARVEST LATER.

Og Mandino

PROBLEMS ARE NOT STOP SIGNS. THEY ARE GUIDELINES.

Robert H. Schuller

GO
FOR
IT

YOU ARE
NEVER TOO
OLD TO SET
ANOTHER
GOAL OR
TO DREAM A
NEW DREAM.

Les Brown

ORDINARY ME CAN ACHIEVE SOMETHING EXTRAORDINARY BY GIVING THAT LITTLE BIT EXTRA.

Bear Grylls

Positivity
is contagious

COURAGE IS THE ART OF BEING THE ONLY ONE WHO KNOWS YOU'RE SCARED TO DEATH.

Earl Wilson

STEP BY STEP AND THE THING IS DONE.

CHARLES ATLAS

CREATE THE
KIND OF SELF
THAT YOU WILL
BE HAPPY TO
LIVE WITH ALL
YOUR LIFE.

GOLDA MEIR

You don't need anybody to tell you who you are or what you are. You are what you are.

John Lennon

TAKE THE FIRST STEP IN FAITH. YOU DON'T HAVE TO SEE THE WHOLE STAIRCASE. JUST TAKE THE FIRST STEP.

Martin Luther King Jr

Only Joy
have the
power
to change
Your future

EVERYONE'S DREAM CAN COME TRUE iF YOU JUST STICK TO iT AND WORK HARD.

SERENA WILLIAMS

TAKE THE TIME TO BE

SILLY

Never give in – never, never, never, never.

Winston Churchill

I'M CRAZY AND I DON'T PRETEND TO BE ANYTHING ELSE.

Rihanna

WHAT YOU DO TODAY CAN IMPROVE ALL YOUR TOMORROWS.

Ralph Marston

The higher
you jump,
the closer
you get

PERSEVERANCE IS NOT A LONG RACE; IT IS MANY SHORT RACES ONE AFTER THE OTHER.

WALTER ELLIOT

BiG SHOTS
ARE ONLY
LiTTLE SHOTS
WHO KEEP
SHOOTiNG.

CHRISTOPHER MORLEY

Treat your problems as opportunities

MAN'S CREATIVE STRUGGLE, HIS SEARCH FOR WISDOM AND TRUTH, IS A LOVE STORY.

Iris Murdoch

SET YOUR
GOALS HiGH,
AND DON'T
STOP TiLL YOU
GET THERE.

BO JACKSON

**That is probably
the best way to feel
confident about
yourself – be grateful
and happy for your lot.**

Fearne Cotton

ONE FINDS LIMITS BY PUSHING THEM.

Herbert Simon

IT'S NOT YOUR JOB TO LIKE ME – IT'S MINE.

Byron Katie

EITHER YOU
RUN THE DAY
OR THE DAY
RUNS YOU.

JIM ROHN

MARCH ON,
AND FEAR NOT
THE THORNS,
OR THE
SHARP STONES
ON LIFE'S PATH.

KAHLIL GIBRAN

I CAN,
THEREFORE
I AM.

Simone Weil

IF YOUR DREAMS RUN, CHASE THEM

YOUR TIME IS LIMITED, SO DON'T WASTE IT LIVING SOMEONE ELSE'S LIFE.

Steve Jobs

NOTHING IS
IMPOSSIBLE.
THE WORD
ITSELF
SAYS "I'M
POSSIBLE"!

AUDREY HEPBURN

BELIEVE YOU CAN AND YOU'RE HALFWAY THERE.

Theodore Roosevelt

Your life
is a book:
make every
chapter
count

Start by doing what's necessary; then do what's possible; and suddenly you are doing the impossible.

Anonymous

ONE CAN
NEVER CONSENT
TO CREEP WHEN
ONE FEELS AN
IMPULSE TO SOAR.

HELEN KELLER

WE MUST HAVE
PERSEVERANCE
AND, ABOVE ALL,
CONFIDENCE
IN OURSELVES.

MARIE CURIE

The greatest
unknowns
can become
your biggest
adventures

WHEN YOU HAVE CONFIDENCE, YOU CAN HAVE A LOT OF FUN.

Joe Namath

EVERY DAY
BRINGS
NEW CHOICES.

MARTHA BECK

Whether you come from a council estate or a country estate, your success will be determined by your own confidence.

Michelle Obama

IF YOU'RE PRESENTING YOURSELF WITH CONFIDENCE, YOU CAN PULL OFF PRETTY MUCH ANYTHING.

Katy Perry

TO LOVE ONESELF IS THE BEGINNING OF A LIFELONG ROMANCE.

OSCAR WILDE

To be yourself in a world that is constantly trying to make you something else is the greatest accomplishment.

Ralph Waldo Emerson

Be your
own head
cheerleader

IT'S ALWAYS TOO EARLY TO QUIT.

Norman Vincent Peale

AS SOON AS YOU TRUST IN YOURSELF, THEN YOU WILL KNOW HOW TO LIVE.

JOHANN WOLFGANG VON **GOETHE**

GO
YOU!

ENTHUSIASM MOVES THE WORLD.

Arthur Balfour

THERE'S NOTHiNG YOU CAN'T HANDLE

i'VE FiNALLY STOPPED RUNNiNG AWAY FROM MYSELF. WHO ELSE iS THERE BETTER TO BE?

GOLDIE HAWN

My attitude is that if you push me towards... a weakness... I will turn that perceived weakness into a strength.

Michael Jordan

OPTIMISM IS THE FAITH THAT LEADS TO ACHIEVEMENT.

Helen Keller

IF YOU'RE GOING THROUGH HELL, KEEP GOING.

ANONYMOUS

Be bold
enough
to cross
the line

YOU ARE WHO YOU ARE WHEN NOBODY'S WATCHING.

Stephen Fry

Dream beyond your horizons

SELF-TRUST iS THE FiRST SECRET OF SUCCESS.

RALPH WALDO EMERSON

Always be a first-rate version of yourself, instead of a second-rate version of somebody else.

Judy Garland

DO SOMETHING WONDERFUL. PEOPLE MAY IMITATE IT.

Albert Schweitzer

THE BEST WAY TO GAIN SELF-CONFIDENCE IS TO DO WHAT YOU ARE AFRAID TO DO.

Anonymous

I WAS ALWAYS LOOKING OUTSIDE MYSELF FOR STRENGTH AND CONFIDENCE BUT IT COMES FROM WITHIN.

Anna Freud

IT'S YOURS FOR THE TAKING

You have within you, right now, everything you need to deal with whatever the world can throw at you.

Brian Tracy

KEEP YOUR EYES ON THE STARS, AND YOUR FEET ON THE GROUND.

THEODORE ROOSEVELT

Show
the world
what you're
made of

TO TRUST ONE'S MIND AND TO KNOW THAT ONE IS WORTHY OF HAPPINESS IS THE ESSENCE OF SELF-ESTEEM.

NATHANIEL BRANDEN

LIFE SHRINKS OR EXPANDS IN PROPORTION TO ONE'S COURAGE.

Anaïs Nin

Nothing splendid has ever been achieved except by those who dared believe... something inside of them was superior to circumstance.

Bruce Barton

Never tell yourself "no" before you've even started

I'M DONE COMPROMISING; EVEN MORE SO, I'M DONE WITH BEING COMPROMISED.

Mila Kunis

FOLLOW YOUR PASSION, FOLLOW YOUR HEART, AND THE THINGS YOU NEED WILL COME.

Elizabeth Taylor

THE MOST EFFECTiVE WAY TO DO iT, iS TO DO iT.

AMELIA EARHART

NEVER BEND YOUR HEAD. ALWAYS HOLD IT HIGH. LOOK THE WORLD STRAIGHT IN THE EYE.

HELEN KELLER

PLUNGE BOLDLY INTO THE THICK OF LIFE, AND SEIZE IT WHERE YOU WILL, IT IS ALWAYS INTERESTING.

Johann
Wolfgang
von Goethe

'TISN'T LIFE
THAT MATTERS!
'TIS THE
COURAGE YOU
BRING TO IT.

HUGH WALPOLE

WHY NOT GO OUT ON A LIMB? THAT'S WHERE THE FRUIT IS.

FRANK SCULLY

THE TIDE TURNS AT LOW WATER AS WELL AS AT HIGH.

H. Havelock Ellis

**Find out who you are
and be that person...
Find that truth, live that
truth and everything
else will come.**

Ellen DeGeneres

YOU'RE THE THE BOSS

DARE TO LOVE YOURSELF AS IF YOU WERE A RAINBOW WITH GOLD AT BOTH ENDS.

Aberjhani

PASSION IS ENERGY. FEEL THE POWER THAT COMES FROM FOCUSING ON WHAT EXCITES YOU.

Oprah Winfrey

SELF-CONFIDENCE IS THE FIRST REQUISITE TO GREAT UNDERTAKINGS.

SAMUEL JOHNSON

The only
way out is
by going
forward

HAPPINESS IS THE SECRET TO ALL BEAUTY; THERE IS NO BEAUTY THAT IS ATTRACTIVE WITHOUT HAPPINESS.

Christian Dior

Courage is not the absence of fear, but rather the judgement that something else is more important than fear.

Ambrose Hollingworth Redmoon

FOLLOW YOUR DREAMS

IF MY MIND CAN CONCEIVE IT, AND MY HEART CAN BELIEVE IT, I KNOW I CAN ACHIEVE IT.

JESSE JACKSON

A GREAT LEADER'S COURAGE TO FULFIL HIS VISION COMES FROM PASSION, NOT POSITION.

John Maxwell

A SHIP IN HARBOUR IS SAFE, BUT THAT'S NOT WHAT SHIPS ARE FOR.

JOHN A. SHEDD

Rise
to the
challenge

YOUR WILLINGNESS TO WRESTLE WITH YOUR DEMONS WILL CAUSE YOUR ANGELS TO SING.

August Wilson

Sometimes
you have to
jump hurdles
to win
the race

TOUGHNESS IS IN THE SOUL AND SPIRIT, NOT IN MUSCLES.

Alex Karras

COURAGE IS RESISTANCE TO FEAR, MASTERY OF FEAR – NOT ABSENCE OF FEAR.

Mark Twain

Always bear in mind that your own resolution to succeed is more important than any other one thing.

Abraham Lincoln

BE YOURSELF.
DO WHATEVER
YOU WANT TO
DO AND DON'T
LET BOUNDARIES
HOLD YOU BACK.

SOPHIE TURNER

BE SO GOOD THEY CAN'T IGNORE YOU.

Steve Martin

THERE'S ALWAYS A WAY

BE BRAVE.
TAKE RiSKS.
NOTHiNG CAN
SUBSTiTUTE
EXPERiENCE.

PAULO COELHO

WITH THE NEW DAY COMES NEW STRENGTH AND NEW THOUGHTS.

Eleanor Roosevelt

NEVER
GIVE UP

The
strongest
steel is
forged in
the hottest
fire

I PROMISE
YOU THAT
EACH AND
EVERY ONE
OF YOU
IS MADE TO
BE WHO
YOU ARE.

Selena Gomez

You will never do anything in this world without courage. It is the greatest quality of the mind next to honour.

Aristotle

IT'S THE JOB THAT'S NEVER STARTED AS TAKES LONGEST TO FINISH.

J. R. R. Tolkien

IF YOU HAVE AN IDEA, YOU HAVE TO BELIEVE IN YOURSELF OR NO ONE ELSE WILL.

Sarah Michelle Gellar

Goals
are only
achievable
once you
set them

Happiness is a matter of one's most ordinary and everyday mode of consciousness being busy and lively and unconcerned with self.

Iris Murdoch

PERSEVERANCE IS FAILING NINETEEN TIMES AND SUCCEEDING THE TWENTIETH.

JULIE ANDREWS

SOMETIMES
COURAGE IS THE
QUIET VOICE AT
THE END OF THE
DAY SAYING,
"I WILL
TRY AGAIN
TOMORROW."

MARY ANNE RADMACHER

SHOW YOUR DOUBTS WHAT YOU'RE MADE OF

NEVER GIVE UP! FAILURE AND REJECTION ARE ONLY THE FIRST STEP TO SUCCEEDING.

Jim Valvano

CHAMPIONS KEEP PLAYING UNTIL THEY GET IT RIGHT.

BILLIE JEAN KING

Your chances of success in any undertaking can always be measured by your belief in yourself.

Robert Collier

You're
unstoppable!

EVERY MORNING STARTS A NEW PAGE IN YOUR STORY. MAKE IT A GREAT ONE TODAY.

Doe Zantamata

SUCCESS
SEEMS TO
BE LARGELY
A MATTER OF
HANGING ON
AFTER OTHERS
HAVE LET GO.

William
Feather

NOTHING CAN DIM THE LIGHT WHICH SHINES FROM WITHIN.

Maya Angelou

WE HAVE A HOPE
OF SUCCEEDING
IF WE LEARN
FROM OUR
PAST MISTAKES.

CARL LEVIN

SUCCESS IS NOT FINAL, FAILURE IS NOT FATAL: IT IS THE COURAGE TO CONTINUE THAT COUNTS.

Winston Churchill

THiS ABOVE ALL: TO THiNE OWN SELF BE TRUE.

WILLIAM SHAKESPEARE

DEFEAT iS NOT THE WORST OF FAILURES. NOT TO HAVE TRIED iS THE TRUE FAILURE.

GEORGE EDWARD WOODBERRY

BE
YOUR
BEST

SHOOT FOR THE MOON. EVEN IF YOU MISS, YOU'LL LAND AMONG THE STARS.

Les Brown

HE WHO MOVES NOT FORWARD, GOES BACKWARD.

JOHANN WOLFGANG VON GOETHE

THERE IS NO GREATER THING YOU CAN DO WITH YOUR LIFE AND YOUR WORK THAN FOLLOW YOUR PASSIONS.

Richard Branson

CHASE
YOUR
DREAMS

I DON'T THINK LIMITS.

USAIN BOLT

IF YOU RISK NOTHING YOU GAIN NOTHING.

Bear Grylls

IF YOU CAN FIND A PATH WITH NO OBSTACLES, IT PROBABLY DOESN'T LEAD ANYWHERE.

Frank A. Clark

You can
do it!

WE NEED TO BE CONFIDENT. WE NEED NOT TO BLINK.

SEBASTIAN COE

WE NEED
TO LEARN
TO LOVE
OURSELVES
FIRST, IN ALL
OUR GLORY
AND OUR
IMPERFECTIONS.

John Lennon

BEWARE; FOR i
AM FEARLESS,
AND THEREFORE
POWERFUL.

MARY SHELLEY

IF YOU FELL DOWN YESTERDAY, STAND UP TODAY.

H. G. WELLS

I WANT TO BE REMEMBERED AS THE GIRL WHO STOOD UP.

Malala Yousafzai

For more information about
our books, find us on Facebook
at **Summersdale Publishers**
and follow us on Twitter
at **@Summersdale**.

www.summersdale.com